GIDEON - A YELLOW LAB

(A LOVE STORY)

NINA B. MARINO & LEE ANN B. MARINO

GIDEON – A YELLOW LAB
(A LOVE STORY)

NINA B. MARINO
ILLUSTRATIONS BY: LEE ANN B. MARINO

Published by:

Happiness House Books

(An imprint of The Righteous Pen
Publications Group)
www.righteouspenpublications.com

ISBN: 1-940197-51-1
13-Digit: 978-1-940197-51-7

Printed in the United States of America.

ABOUT THIS BOOK

The feature star of our story, Gideon, is a yellow Labrador Retriever. At the time of our original publication, he was 10 years old. Featured in some of the photos are his owner and caretaker since he was a nine-week-old puppy, Lee Ann Marino. For about seven years of his life, Gideon lived with a condition known as Canine Dementia. Similar to Alzheimer's Disease in humans, Canine Dementia causes disorientation, sleep disruption, confusion, forgetfulness, lack of response when they are called, and anxiety in dogs. In later stages, it can cause disruption in bladder and bowel habits, and dogs may no longer bark, recognize their owners, or recognize their names. Although it's not very well known, it is not an uncommon illness in older dogs. Unfortunately, at this time, there are few treatments for Canine Dementia. The medical options that do exist cause serious side effects. That means pet owners who experience the sting of Canine Dementia in their beloved pets find ways to take care of them, comfort them, and create consistent schedules and environments until the time when they can no longer care for their pets.

Our beloved Gideon passed away in September of 2022. This story was written to honor his life, as he was a great pet and a faithful companion. This book serves as a memory book for him, now that he is no longer with us. We also write this notation with the hope to promote information and education about Canine Dementia. If you suspect your pet displays signs of this disorder, there is a wealth of information available on the internet and through your local vet.

Even though pets live with us for only a short while, we know they live on in our hearts forever. Beloved pets are an important part of our lives. This story is about Gideon, but can stand to be about any dog or any pet, told in a fashion that children can enjoy. We hope you enjoy it as much as we enjoyed Gideon throughout his 14 years of life.

Gideon was born on a wonderful farm in
Indiana. His mother was yellow, his
father was black. Out of nine puppies,
Gideon was the only yellow lab.

Gideon was sweet.
Gideon was cute.
Gideon was cuddly,
and...

Gideon was "little."

Gideon was a great puppy.
He was warm.
He was fuzzy,
and...

He was "little."

Gideon grew.

He had big, beautiful,
almond-shaped brown eyes.
He had soft, floppy ears.
He had soft, golden fur,
and...

He was "little."

Gideon loved to play.

He loved to play tug of war.
His favorite toy
was an old pair of stockings.
He loved to play ball in the park,
and…

He was "little."

Gideon loved laying
on the big, green couch.
He loved snuggling
in the big, green stuffed chair.
He loved his pillow and blanket.

Gideon loved bananas,
apples, and carrots.
He loved drinking water
and going outside.

Gideon was little…

Gideon grew in size and became a great
pet and friend.
He loved his owner, Lee Ann.
They played, romped
and went for walks together, always.
They had a wonderful time together,
and...

Gideon was "little."

Gideon was Lee Ann's baby boy.
He loved to sit in her lap.
He loved to sit at her feet.
He always found peace
and safety in her presence.
He was her baby,
and...

He was "little."

Gideon grew older now.
It got harder to get him
to chase the ball.
It got harder to get him to take a bath
(he hates baths).
His place of safety remains
in Lee Ann's lap,
Or at her feet,
for...

He is "Little."

No matter how old he gets,
Gideon still loves to be a lap puppy
And have his belly rubbed.

He lays in Lee Ann's lap still,
just like a baby,
For no matter how old he gets,
Gideon will forever remain…

"Little."

Gideon playing in the snow, January 2017

ABOUT THE AUTHOR

Nina B. Marino, affectionately known as "Gideon's grandma," is a Registered Nurse and Legal Nurse Consultant. She was involved in the nursing profession for over 40 years and in legal nurse consulting for over 20. Nina also works and operates in Christian ministry. Within the Kingdom of God, Nina is a prophet and intercessor. She is an original founding member of Sanctuary International Fellowship Tabernacle (SIFT) in Charlotte, North Carolina, where she serves as an elder.

Nina has loved the written word for a long time, especially reading and sharing books with children. Her work with children has spanned as a mother, grandmother, school nurse, and childhood educator for well over 60 years. She loves crafting and cooking, and, of course, pets and pet ownership. In her crafting work, she is a designer for Rose of Sharon Creations. To learn more about Nina, visit www.roseofsharoncreations.com.

ABOUT THE ILLUSTRATOR

Lee Ann B. Marino, also known as "Gideon's mom," is a full-time minister, author, professor, editor, and publisher. She is an author of over 35 titles and has been involved with Christian ministry for over 25 years and serves as a licensed and ordained minister of the Gospel, serving in her own ministry, Sanctuary Apostolic Fellowship Empowerment (SAFE). She is also founder and Overseer of Sanctuary International Fellowship Tabernacle (SIFT) in

Charlotte, North Carolina and The Sanctuary Network. Within the Kingdom of God, Lee Ann serves in the ministry office of apostle. She is host of the *Kingdom Now* podcast and also serves as Chancellor for Apostolic Covenant Theological Seminary (ACTS).

Lee Ann is honored to celebrate the life of her dog, Gideon, in this children's book by providing all the photographs, converted to painting-like illustrations, throughout this work. She was a pet owner to two Labrador Retrievers, Gideon and Fiona, for over 14 years. She loves pets and pet ownership, crafting, and sewing. In her crafting work, she is a designer for Rose of Sharon Creations and in her publishing work, Editor-in-Chief for Righteous Pen Publications. To learn more about Lee Ann, visit www.kingdompowernow.org.

www.ingramcontent.com/pod-product-compliance
Lightning Source LLC
Chambersburg PA
CBHW041553040426
42447CB00002B/175